T0086447

PHILOSOPHY

HEGELIAN DIALECTIC & DEMOCRATIZATION PROCESS:

Understanding the Two Philosophical Concepts

JONATHAN KATHENGE, PhD. MBA.

authorHOUSE®

AuthorHouse™
1663 Liberty Drive
Bloomington, IN 47403
www.authorhouse.com
Phone: 1 (800) 839-8640

Published by AuthorHouse 10/16/2017

ISBN: 978-1-5462-1255-3 (sc)
ISBN: 978-1-5462-1256-0 (e)

Library of Congress Control Number: 2017915623

Print information available on the last page.

Contents

Dedication

To my grandparents, men and women of great political sagacity; and for all those who will dedicate their time to read and think through the thoughts reflected here.

Preface

This book came into being as a result of my in depth study of Hegel. As I reflected on his ideas, I became interested in understanding how his concept of dialectic triad continues to shape our national politics today. In this book I have discussed two issues from the point of view advanced by philosophers and socio-political ideologists, that is; Hegel's concept of dialectic principle commonly referred to as Hegelian dialectic and its inter-relationship with the concept of democratization process. I begin from ancient philosophers prior to Hegel to where Hegel picked up the idea of dialectic reasoning and go through its historical development for the purpose of presenting a clear understanding and historical overview of the concept. The connection between the two discussed concepts, that is; democracy and dialectic has basis from Hegel's main political work "Philosophy of Right". Though in this work Hegel is not specific on democracy, he does allude to it and admittedly defend representative institutions, constitution and basic rights. Moreover, in his lectures before the publication of "Philosophy of Right", He discusses the principle of opposition (Hegel, 1974: 707-709), and in the "Philosophy of Right" he conceived the State basically in

ix

terms of unity. According to him, conflicts appear at the level of the civil society where parochial aims are pursued; nevertheless, they are superseded and reconciled rationally at the level of the State where disagreements are solved by rational communication, a process better understood from dialectic perspective. The importance of this book cannot be over stated as a reflection on the question; "What has been the effect on society for 200 years of Hegelian dialectic since ancient to modern times?"

Introduction

An examination of the history of philosophy shows that the great age of scholastic philosophy was an outcome of the reforms of the eleventh century. The reaction to the reforms evolved to modern philosophy, and conflicts of different philosophies continue to evolve in the thoughts of the twenty first century (Russel, 1972). Therefore, it can be argued that without insight into the philosophy of the earlier centuries, the intellectual atmosphere of the twenty first century can hardly be understood. I am of the opinion that an understanding of Hegelian dialectic will shed more light into the history of philosophy. To ascertain this, I systematically in this book go through historical development of the Hegelian dialectic principle in relation to the times that informed Hegel's thought and the times that it has helped to form. In an attempt to cover at great length the historical dimension of the Hegelian theory of dialectics, it became necessary to be selective on what and whose views to take into account from the existing pool of philosophers. I arguably elevate Hegel's philosophical merit against other philosophers of his time such as, John Lock, Jacques Rousseau, George Bryon, John Dewey and William James as well as other idealists, empiricists, utilitarian and pragmatists. Hegel left legacy of all times as an idealist philosopher. Hegel significantly distinguishes himself by keeping a key theme in his dialectic principle: that is, oneness or unity of the triad movement for his thesis, antithesis, and Synthesis concept. In the second section of the book, I have picked democratization process to advance an analysis of Hegelian dialectic as a common ideology.

CHAPTER 1

The Dialectic System

Dialectic is a system of reasoning put forth by modern philosopher Georg Wilhelm Hegel. His philosophy of history greatly impacted on modern political landscape during his time and after through his students. According to Hegel's dialectic thought, all historical developments follow three basic laws: First, each event follows a necessary course; this implies that an event could not have happened in any other way. Secondly, each historical event represents not only change but progress from the previous status. Thirdly, one historical event or trend tends to be replaced by its opposite, which is later replaced by its opposite, which is later replaced by a resolution of the two extremes in a progressive development (Wilhelm, 1956).

The third law of Hegel's basic laws is dialectically expressed as; "Each historical event or trend tends to be replaced by its opposite, which is later replaced by a resolution of the two extremes as if mediating the extremes in a progressive continuum known in sciences as pendulum theory (T.M Knox & Pelcyzynsky, 1964). Pendulum theory in sciences

1

has been used by historians to explain how events swing from one extreme to the other before the pendulum comes to rest at the middle. Hegel and his students also explained the dialectic using Isaac Newton's first and third laws of motion. Isaac Newton's first law of motion states that; every-body persists in its state of being at rest or keeps moving uniformly straight forward except in so far as it is compelled to change its state by force. Pre- Socratic Philosopher Parmenides had called this a state of permanence, in his philosophy of cosmology. Newton's third law of motion states that: to every action there is always an equal and opposite reaction. Hegel and his followers named the extreme phases of these laws, which happen progressively as thesis and antithesis, and called the resolution a synthesis. It is on the Bases of this dialectic reasoning that Hegel argued that human beings can comprehend the unfolding of history (Wilhelm, 1956). This is closely understood through the principle of sufficient reason which states that; present events have connection with previous ones, and according to the principle of self-evident truth, a thing cannot come into existence without a cause.

Hegel in his work on dialectics postulated that one can get a commanding grasp of the world in which he lives by understanding its roots in the past, and the forces of change and development now working within it (Lavine, 1984). He introduced the discussion on his viewpoint on dialectic concept in the preface of his work "The Phenomenology of Spirit" translated from German "Phanomenologie des Geistes", also called "Phenomenology of Mind" or the Experience of consciousness. To begin this most celebrated work, he talked about the history of philosophy as a crucial part of the biography of human spirit. Hegel points out that in the history of Philosophy opposing philosophical systems compete and struggle with each other, each claiming to have found the exclusive, one and only truth, each denying any truth to the opponent. From a dialectical perspective, what Hegel argues here is affirmed by study on the history of philosophy. Through the study of history of philosophy, we observe bitter enmities between philosophers for their ideas from which emerge conflicting philosophies in the form of thesis, antithesis, and synthesis. It begins with the philosophies of Heraclitus against Parmenides, Plato against Sophists, Descartes against the Empiricists, the Catholic Scholastics and Hume against Descartes, Kant against Hume. The line continues to African against Western philosophers to the pragmatists against Utilitarianisms. However, in his dialectic idealism, Hegel asserts that the disagreement between the various philosophers and their philosophies, when adequately understood, illustrates not conflict but the growth and development of truth. That is, from Hegelian dialectic perspective, differing philosophical systems should not be viewed as at war with one another but as elements of an organic unity. Viewed from this perspective, each philosophy has significance as a stage in the development of philosophy. As such, no philosophy is false, as each is a necessary part of the organic growth and unity of all philosophy. Therefore, each stage in the development displaces the other, but they do not falsify each other. According to Hegel, each is a necessary stage in the development of the whole truth, of the dialectical manifestation or revelation of absolute spirit to the growth of the finite, human spirit, or consciousness of the mind.

The invisible dialectic within existential situations or groupings controls the process of the conflict and the resolution of differences, and leads everyone involved into a circle of conflicts (Friedrich, 2012). The dialectic can be advanced as a Philosophical approach that in principle explains how human beings progress towards a better and more egalitarian condition; but pragmatically provides the political elite a strategy for controlling the society. Hegel postulated that each human development and course of human history is driven by an argument, which at a certain point in the process is re-started. According to Hegel, this dialectic process can explain everything, including art, culture, history, and even nature (Hegel, 155).

Causality and Hegelian Dialectic

Under the principle of sufficient reason, present events have a connection with previous ones. That is, according to this principle also known as the principle of self- evident truth, a thing cannot come into existence without a cause. Based on this principle, imaginary causes have been gradually pushed out of the way as the boundaries of our knowledge continue to expand, and they would probably completely vanish in the face of sound Philosophy which sees in them only the expression of our present ignorance of the true causes. For instance, using dialectic concept, the proponents of Hegelian dialectic would argue that; the capitalistic elites can create a constant conflict with communists and socialists for economic purpose. To achieve this goal all they need is fabricate a reason in order to get the backing or support of the larger public behind their hidden motive. Therefore, they create a problem; the media react and give a communist or socialist as somebody whom to blame; the public react; consequently a solution is offered as war on communism or socialism. The public buy this idea, enabling the elite get their way and own the solution. This concept is based on the principle of sufficient reason which Hegel adapted in his dialectic concept to argue that there is no such thing as coincidence. He pointed out that we can critically analyze and explain the remote as well as proximate cause of every historical event, from the French revolution to the current trends shaping each particular government or society in the world today.

CHAPTER 2

The Development of Dialectics Concept in the History of Philosophy

Introduction

This chapter gives background and an overview about the historical development of dialectic concept within the philosophical cycles. It identifies the fragments of Hegelian dialectic from the dialogues of ancient philosophers to the contemporary times. It also points out how the concept has been discussed and developed by philosophers and other academicians addressing the modern day issues confronting the society and man's existential situation.

Dialectic is one of the oldest philosophical concepts, with its appearance in very ancient Greek thought more than five hundred years before Hegel. For instance, in ancient Greece, dialectic was a form of reasoning that proceeded by question and answer, as illustrated by the dialogues of Socrates. In the later antiquity and in the middle ages, the term was used to mean simply logic, but Immanuel Kant applied it to arguments showing that principles of Science have contradictory aspects. Hegel thought that all logic and world history itself followed a dialectical path in which internal contradictions were transcended, but gave rise to new contradictions that themselves required resolution. Marx and Engels gave Hegel's idea of dialectic a material basis, the dialectical materialism. These systems and their historical developments on the dialectic concept will be discussed in this chapter.

ANCIENT PERIOD

Heraclitus and Parmenides

Parmenides (late sixth or early fifth century B.C) was a pre-Socratic Greek philosopher from Elea. He argued that reality, what he called 'what is', is one, change is impossible, and existence is timeless, uniform, necessary, and unchanging. He pointed out that in the world of appearances, one's sensory faculty lead to conceptions which are deceitful.

Heraclitus, a Greek philosopher of Ephesus (500 BC) came in to counter the arguments of Parmenides with the argument that everything is constantly changing.

Close to the time of Socrates, Heraclitus wrote that all is strife, everything turns into its opposite. Heraclitus argued that everything in reality is in process, in flux, is changing. He used a metaphor to express this flux, that is; 'one cannot bath in the same river/ water twice since it is endlessly

7

flowing, changing, moving with fresh water' (Lavine, 1984). He also used his other famous metaphor 'war is the father of all changes'. A concept heavily borrowed by later philosophers to illustrate the fact that conflict brings change in the triadic movement.

Parmenides, a philosopher of Heraclitus time argued that nothing changes. Parmenides denied any process or development in the world and argued that truth is unchanging and is known only by reason (Lavine, 1984).

Developing dialectic concept from the two ancient philosophers, Hegel argued that Parmenides and Heraclitus created two goal posts which he came to mediate upon. He called the concept of Heraclitus the thesis and that of Parmenides the antithesis. He later took the writings of St. Thomas on causality that taught that everything that moves is moved by another and Isaac Newton's law of motion as thesis based on Heraclitus change and antithesis of Parmenides' permanence to build his synthesis as a dialectical process.

The Sophists

Ancient Philosophers, the sophists (5th Century, B.C), provided a basis for the art of perpetuating dialectic persuasion. The sophists were philosophers from many different societies outside Greece who travelled about from city to city. In the fifth century, they arrived in Athens where they made a reputation as teachers of rhetoric, the art of making persuasive public speeches which was useful for achieving success in politics in democratic Athens where debate in public assembly was open to all citizens (Lavine, 1984). The most famous representatives of the sophistic movements are Protagoras, Gorgias, Antiphon, Hippias, Prodicus and Thrasymachus.

Prior to the fifth Century B.C, virtue or excellence was predominantly associated with the aristocratic warrior virtues such as courage and physical strength. With the coming of the sophists in Athens, virtue or excellence was increasingly understood in terms of the ability to influence one's fellow citizens in political gatherings through rhetorical persuasion. The sophistic education and dialectic influence grew out of this situation and exploited this paradigm shift. This art of persuasion has been used in dialectic debate since the time of the sophists to move a community from one position or ideology to another in politics as well as in the business practice, as it will be attested later.

Socrates

Socrates (469-399 BC), in his philosophy sought to shake us out of our comfortable preoccupations by challenging us to give a rational account of the concepts and categories we employ, often unreflectively, in our ordinary lives. His chief technique was a kind of grueling cross-examination designed to bring out instabilities or inconsistencies in an opponent's position. Many of his dialogues were aimed to show the difficulty of providing a clear definition of what is meant by such notions as justice, friendship, piety, temperance or courage. As a result of Socrates remorseless logical probing, the other participant in the dialogue would be left in a state of confusion, which forces him or her to admit that he or she is unable to give a clear rational account of his or her ordinary beliefs and convictions.

By use of this technique, Socrates himself meant by dialectic, the use of argument in order to make the opponent contradict himself in the course of what came to be known as the Socratic method (Lavine,1984). With this result, Socrates would then resolve the contradiction and be able to move to a true definition of the concept.

Plato

Plato (B.C 428- 348) is regarded as the founder of Western Philosophy and associated with Socrates who was his teacher. His philosophical works were on systematic examination of the nature of human understanding, the foundations of knowledge and the way to achieve excellence in our lives. His philosophy aimed to replace the uncertainties and confusions of ordinary opinion with something more solid and reliable. He sought to provide a clear account of what makes the results of an exercise to qualify as genuine knowledge.

Plato meant by dialectic the highest level of knowledge, a stage in which opposition or contradiction has been overcome. Plato equated dialectic with his idea of reason as the highest faculty of knowledge. To demonstrate how human beings dialectically move in their knowledge, which is lacking on average citizens of the state, he used the example of the Athenians. In his theory of knowledge, using an example of Athenians on their understanding of democracy, Plato demonstrated that the average Athenian could supply, if questioned, a roughly adequate description of the democratic government which affects them personally. But such a person would be unable to identify the principles on which the government is based, or the traits an ideal government should have (Plato: The Republic, Book VI).

Benedict Spinoza

Benedict Spinoza (1632-1677) one of the greatest philosophers in the early modern period was born to an immigrant Jewish family in Amsterdam. He argues that all mental and physical phenomena are modes of a single all-embracing substance, that is, 'God or Nature'. He unfolds his metaphysical system through a series of meticulous geometrical demonstrations, but with his chief interest being to apply it to human life. He describes how a rational understanding of the inescapable causes of all phenomena can enable us to master the passions and make the transition from servitude to freedom.

Benedict Spinoza associated dialectic with causality. He argued that experience, no less clearly than reason, amply shows that the only reason people believe themselves free is that they are conscious of their actions, while being unaware of the causes that determine them. The decisions of the mind are nothing but its appetites, which vary depending on the various states of the body. Our own emotions are the basis for all the decisions we take; those of us afflicted by contrary emotions do not know what we want, while if no emotion is present, it takes but a slight impulse to drive us in one direction or another (Curley, 1985).

Immanuel Kant

Immanuel Kant (1724-1804) was born in Koningsberg, East Prussia where he also became a professor of Logic and Metaphysics. His philosophical reflections gave rise to philosophical debates of early modern period over the source and foundations of human knowledge, and subsequent conceptions of the scope and nature of philosophical inquiry.

Kant's dialectic influence can be traced in his reflections on duty and reason as the ultimate principle in his work, 'Groundwork of the Metaphysic of Morals'. This work is significantly a synthesis of utilitarian, a normative theory in ethics propagated by John Stuart Mill, and pragmatic, a theory of practical conceptions advanced by William James. Kant called his theory of morals in this debate a categorical imperative. He picks his starting point as a distinction between what is good merely as means to an end, and what is intrinsically good, or good in itself. In his debate on the categorical imperative, Kant dialectically provides necessary rather than sufficient condition for morality and rules out certain maxims which cannot in reason be universally adopted. In arguing for the intrinsic value of a good will, he provided a cornerstone for morality by locating the source of moral value in the autonomous will of the rational agent. This leads to a new version of the categorical imperative, that is; 'Act in such a way that you always treat humanity, whether in your own person or in that of any other, never simply as means, but always at the same time as an end. This principle of respect for persons has since come to be recognized as of enormous importance for morality. His argument is based on a moral vision where no one is simply used as means to the furtherance of someone else's projects, but each human being accords to all other humans the right to respect as rational, self-determining agent (Cottingham, 2008). Kant influenced the thinking of Hegel as an idealist. In his dialectic arguments on ethics where he discusses the problem of evil of which treating others as means rather than ends is seen as an evil in Kant's categorical imperative perspective. Borrowing from Kantian ethics, Hegel calls history slaughter bench of morals meaning that throughout historical epochs, ethical values have been periodically eroded. He clarifies this by stating,

"History is the slaughter- bench at which the happiness of peoples, the wisdom of States, and the virtue of individuals have been victimized" (Lavine, 1984: 288).

Hegel

Georg Wilhelm Friedrich Hegel (1770-1831), was born in Stuttgart Germany. His academic career culminated to his appointment as Professor of Philosophy in Berlin. He is famous for his dialectic theory according to which all actual events in the world can be seen as stages in the progressive development of full self-conscious rationality; the absolute Mind, or 'self-positing' Spirit. According to Hegel, self-knowledge is the goal or end towards which the entire world system is moving, and the self-conscious cognitive activities of human beings are in a certain sense the culmination of that process. Hegel stresses the importance of historical dimension of all human activities. He argued that the development of human thought has to be understood as a continuous dynamic process, in which each stage arises from the struggle to overcome the limitations of what has gone before (Cottingham, 2008).

Like Aristotle and St. Thomas Aquinas before him, Hegel tried to develop a comprehensive philosophy as separate area of study and was interested in the history of ideas in many fields besides philosophy. He believed that various philosophical systems represented different stages in the development of the human spirit, this led him to hold that reality is constantly changing, a position previously held by Heraclitus. Further to this belief, Hegel held that everything carries its own contradiction within itself. He asserted that all things have a plus and a minus which are in constant battle, and through their struggle create higher and more complex pluses and minuses (Kamau, 2014). Thesis, antithesis, synthesis is one way of expressing the pluses and minuses and their eventual union. The law of growth, for Hegel, was the struggle between opposites. It is upon this premise Hegel developed his dialectic concept, in addition to reflecting upon the dialectical theories of earlier philosophers.

Hegel's Dialectic concept

Hegel distinguished himself from earlier philosophers on the concept of dialectic by his clarity on the idea of the dialectic, which he referred to as a triadic movement. He illustrated his dialectic concept through a triadic movement which consists of; thesis, antithesis, and synthesis. He based this triadic movement on the underlying assumption of the traditional logic which assumes that every proposition has a subject and a predicate. According to this view, every fact consists in something having some property. That is, from an empirical point of view, since everything, except the whole, has relations to the outside things; it follows that, nothing quite true can be said about separate things, and that, in fact, only the whole is real. This explains according to Hegel the triadic or dialectic movement of the parts towards the whole or the absolute. This follows more directly from the fact that to say 'A and B are two' from logical point of view is not a subject-predicate proposition. On the basis of traditional logic, there can be no such proposition. There are not as many as two things in the world, the whole considered as a unity, is alone real (Russell, 1972). Hegel used this traditional logic or reasoning in his dialectic to show that we ought to treat each event as a whole in search of truth, with a predicate-proposition mentality. It is not an explicit argument in his concept, but implicit in his reasoning system.

Hegel developed his dialectic concept with logical progression coherently. He begins the argument of his logic by the assumption that 'the absolute is pure being';

we assume that it just is, without assigning any quality to it; –this becomes the thesis. But pure being without any qualities is nothing; therefore we are led to the antithesis-the absolute is 'Nothing'. From this thesis and antithesis we pass on to the synthesis- the union of 'Being' and 'Not-Being' is 'Becoming', and so we say the absolute is becoming (Russell 1972). This is not conclusive either, because there has to be something that becomes. From this perspective, our views of reality develop by the continual correction of previous errors, all of which arose from undue abstraction, by taking something finite or limited as if it could be the whole. This process, according to Hegel is essential to the understanding of the result. Each later stage of the dialectic contains all earlier stages, as it were the solution. According to this reasoning of Hegel, it is therefore impossible to reach the truth except by going through all the steps of the dialectic, because knowledge as a whole has its triadic movement. According to Hegel, truth or knowledge begins with sense perception in which there is only awareness of the object. Through skeptical criticism of the senses, it becomes purely subjective. At last it reaches the stage of self-knowledge in which subject and object are no longer distinct. For Hegel's dialectic, the highest kind of knowledge must be that possessed by the absolute, and the absolute is the whole and there is nothing outside itself for it to know.

According to Hegel, truth and falsehood are not sharply defined opposites as is commonly supposed. Nothing is wholly false, and nothing we can know is wholly true. Later, David Masolo seemed to take note of this in his philosophy of knowledge. Masolo, in his view on truth and knowledge pointed out truth is an opinion and asserted that to be true is to be opined (Masolo, 1994)

Hegel's dialectic theory as a synthesis of earlier philosophers' concepts

In his theory of the dialectic, Hegel says dialectic is a synthesis of the opposites. By this statement Hegel means that, every concept, as we think about it, begins to show us limitations, and passes over into its opposite, into the very negation of itself (Lavine,1984). This is illustrated here by a presentation of his theory compared to those of some early philosophers.

Hegel in comparison to Heraclitus and Parmenides' dialectic concept

Hegel illustrated the theory of his dialectic using the Heraclitus sense of opposition, conflict, polarity or contradiction. The disciples of Heraclitus had argued that it characterizes all human thought. Hegel argued that once Heraclitus' concept is reflected upon, it begins to show its own limitations and it passes over into its very opposite in Parmenides' claim that nothing changes, that reality is eternally what it is.

Plato provided the synthesis for the thesis of Heraclitus and the antithesis of Parmenides. He retained the Heraclitus' concept of change, but confined it to the sensible world. He retained Parmenides concept of unchanging, but confined it to the intelligible world (Lavine, 1984). By doing this, Plato synthesized the thesis and antithesis and took the dialectic development to a higher level from Heraclitus and Parmenides. From Plato's concept, Hegel picked up the dialectic theory and clarified it further. He developed his dialectic theory to a triadic process to consist of three stages or moments of a concept and called it a triadic.

Hegel developed this dialectic theory upon the concepts of Heraclitus and Parmenides. He called the concept of Heraclitus the thesis and that of Parmenides. Parmenides concept arises to oppose Heraclitus concept, the antithesis. As for the synthesis, Hegel developed it from his argument that the conflict or opposition in which thesis and antithesis struggle against each other can be overcome.

When we think through the thesis –antithesis conflict and struggle there must emerge finally a concept which will resolve the conflict, unify the opposing concepts, and retain what is true and valuable in each of them (Lavine, 1984). This third concept Hegel called the synthesis. This is an idea that has been borrowed for a long time as a conflict resolution mechanism to build consensus among opposing camps or groups especially in the political field.

An elaborate illustration of Hegel's triadic is found in his expression of the dialectic process. That is, the process of dialectic moves from a first stage or moment (the thesis) to a second stage or moment which negates, opposes, or contradicts the first (the antithesis); and this opposition is overcome by a third stage in which a new concept (the synthesis) emerges as a higher truth which transcends them (Lavine, 1984). The functions of the dialectic are:

(i) to cancel the conflict between thesis and antithesis
(ii) to preserve or retain the element of truth within the thesis and antithesis
(iii) to transcend the opposition and raise up or sublimate the conflict into a higher truth.

This triadic process of dialectic is not limited to history of philosophy, it is rather a rhythm of all reality which. According to Hegel, the rational conceptual truths which underlie all the areas of human experience and knowledge are not static, but in dialectical movement from thesis to opposing antithesis to reconciling synthesis. The whole of what is known at particular historical period is just what the absolute mind has dialectically revealed, its manifestation at that particular point (Hegel, 1956).

Hegel and Plato's dialectic theories

A comparison between Hegel and Plato's dialectic theories shows varying differences. That is:

(i) For Plato, dialectic as the highest level of knowledge has as its goal as the removal of contradictions. For Hegel the contradiction can never be overcome, the generation of contradiction or opposites and their synthesis is the very nature of rational thought and of reality itself.

(ii) For Plato, dialectic yields the immutable static truth of the forms. For Hegel dialectic yields the dynamically changing truths of the concepts. Thus, dialectical reason moves continuously through tension, opposition, conflict and contradiction towards resolution to synthesis. Hegel differs with Plato on dialectical reason because Plato's view perceives pure forms in their identity and their interrelatedness.

(iii) For Plato dialectic yields forms or ideas which are rational and timeless, derived not from the visible but from the intelligible world and they represent a transcendent realm of truth. For Hegel conceptual truth is imminent in existent things, in the changing process of the world and is time bound.

Despite the above pointed differences between Plato and Hegel on the dialectic theory, a close look into their theories reveal significant agreements. That is:

(i) Both regard dialectic as the highest level of knowledge. According to their theory, the dialectic seeks to grasp reality in the form of underlying rational conceptual truth. They both review their idealism in that they regard dialectic as superior and more profound approach to reality than sense perception which is an empirical approach to reality or the method of understanding with which science operates.

(ii) Both Hegel and Plato through a dialectic method construct arrive at a major totalizing philosophy in which rational concepts organize and synthesize all aspects of reality into a single, interconnected and meaningful whole. By so doing they developed philosophy to a higher level of knowledge in the understanding of the universe and human existence.

Hegel distinguishes himself as a master of dialectic among his predecessors and peers by his clarity in illustrating dialectic as both an essential character of reality itself and the method for understanding reality. That is, we can only understand reality in its constant conflict and change and as a process in a triadic movement. Dialectic understood in this context is both a rhythmic movement of all human thought and history and the method for understanding them (Lavine, 1984). In his dialectic, as an idealist Hegel contends that the highest state of man can only be attained through ideological conflict and resolution. To this end, Hegel's dialectic explains the reasoning behind the use of military power to export an illogical version of freedom and false democratic ideas (Cottingham, 2008).

Hegel postulated that one can get commanding grasp of the world in which he or she lives by understanding its roots in the past, and the forces of change and development now working within it. Hegel develops this theme in his masterpiece, "The Phenomenology of Spirit", which tries to understand the human spirit of the present time by looking back at its development, and at its roots in the past. Hegel's book, "Phenomenology of Spirit", presents a biography, not of particular person, but of spirit of humanity over the long centuries as it develops, grows, matures in its striving, values, and philosophizing. He introduces the dialectic concept by presenting to the minds all the world views, religious faiths, and Philosophic visions that human beings have held and the truths they claim to have discovered. He proceeds to show the kind of persons who hold these views and under what circumstances, then goes to show how each Philosophy in the history of the human spirit, when it is reflected upon and lived with, reveals its own limitations. Thus, each shows itself to be only a partial truth, one-sided, distorted and inadequate. This indicates that each philosophy, world view and religious faith is unstable, tipsy, fallible, and finite. As a result, each stage of its development passes over dialectically into an opposite viewpoint which presents the other side of the issue, basing itself upon what the other view left out. However, in time this opposing viewpoint will also be seen to be limited, partial, and one-sided in its negation of the first philosophy and a new viewpoint will emerge which will synthesize the two opposing philosophies into a more complete truth. Afterwards, the new synthesizing viewpoint will in time arise to assert its deficiencies, and so on, until an all-embracing, all- inclusive vision of total reality is attained (Lavine, 1984).

Karl Marx

Coming soon after Hegel in the dialectic debate was Karl Marx. Karl Marx (1818-1883) was the son of a wealthy Jewish lawyer. He studied in Bonn and Berlin- Germany and later went to Paris- France. Together with Friedrich Engels, they published the Manifesto of the Communist Party in 1849. Marx advanced a world view of the society according to which economic conditions control the direction of history; and the entire superstructure of religious, philosophical and artistic ideas are determined by the economic base. According to him, the struggle is between economic classes, and it's a struggle which could only be resolved by the advent of communism.

Karl Marx took the dialectic of Hegel further giving it an economic and social-political world-view on inquiry based upon a materialistic interpretation of historical development. He built upon it a dialectical view of social change, and an analysis of class relations within society. With use of the dialectic, he gave an analysis and critique of the development of capitalism (Encyclopedia of Philosophy, Vol. II). Marxism dialectic is based on a materialistic understanding of social development, taking its starting point the necessary economic activities required by human society to provide for its material needs. The form of economic organization or mode of production is understood to be the basis from which the majority of other social phenomena; including social relations, political and legal systems, morality and ideology arise. Marx says this dialectic movement is due to class conflict within capitalism which arises due to intensifying contradictions between highly productive mechanized and socialized production performed by the proletariat. It is propelled by private ownership and private appropriation of the surplus product in the form of surplus value by a small minority of private owners called the bourgeoisie. This concept represents an historical development of dialectical movement with capitalism as thesis, socialism as antithesis and communism as synthesis. Marx accepted Hegel's general views but he was particularly interested in social conditions and with the struggle between different classes. He was dissatisfied with Hegel's idealism, and adapted his thinking to materialistic philosophy. From his antithetical position to Hegel he developed a synthesis of a new philosophy which became known as communism, which is the basic political philosophy of Russia.

Karl Popper

Karl Popper famously opposed Marxism in general and its philosophical core, that is, the Marxist dialectic in particular. As a progressive thinker, Popper saw in dialectic a source of dogmatism damaging to philosophy and political theory. He accused advocates of Marxist dialectic of not tolerating criticism. Popper gave the following definition of dialectic;

"dialectic is a theory which maintains that something, for instance, human thought, develops in a way characterized by the so called dialectic triad: thesis, antithesis, synthesis" (Popper, 2002: 412).

This differed from the definition given by materialistic dialectics proponents, that is;

"Dialectics is the method of reasoning which aims to understand things concretely in all their movement, change and interconnection, with their opposite and contradictory sides in unity" (Encyclopaedia of Marxism).

Popper presents trial and error method as a universal way in which human thought in general and scientific development in particular occurs, and compares it with dialectic. According to him, dialectical approaches, though applicable in some situations, do not hold in general. He asserts that although dialectics satisfactorily describes some developments, it is not consistent with others. He supports his claim by four scenarios;

a) When the Thesis and Antithesis do not lead to Synthesis, instead one of them is simply eliminated.

b) Many independent Thesis can be offered, therefore Trial and Error method has wider application than dialectics which does not account for that.

c) The Thesis does not produce Antithesis, rather our critical attitude produces the Antithesis, and sometimes the Antithesis is not produced at all.

d) In the case when the Synthesis is produced, it is not simply a construction built merely of material supplied by Thesis and Antithesis and preserving the best parts of both, if the will contain some entirely new idea.

Therefore, Popper concludes;

"The dialectical interpretation, even where it may be applicable, will hardly ever help to develop thought by its suggestion that a synthesis should be constructed out of the ideas contained in a thesis and antithesis" (Popper, 2002).

Jean Paul- Sartre

Jean Paul Sartre (1905-1980) was a French philosopher, novelist and playwright whose ideas have been a formative influence on twentieth-century culture. He was an existentialist philosopher. In his existentialist outlook, he emphasizes the inescapable anguish of human existence in which we are '*condemned to be free*'.

Sartre's dialectic debate is largely found in his '*Critic of Dialectical Reason*' which is an examination of Marxist views of society. In his dialectic debate, Sartre argues that: Free, independent conscious being, being- for- itself in its concrete existence disappears into his version of Marxist proletariat. The existentialism of conscious being, of the solitary, defiantly free for-itself disappears into his version of the objectivist. Materialistic philosophy of mature Marxism, then disappear into a scientific scenario of the dialectic of history as the struggle of social groupings to overcome scarcity (Lavine, 1984).

Sartre was a follower of Hegel and Marx in dialectic philosophy in that he synthesized their dialectic philosophies. Hegel argued that all philosophies are relative to, and bound to their own historical times. He believed that his own philosophy was bringing the history of philosophy to its inescapable dialectical completion. Marx argued that all philosophies are ideologies, reflections of the dominant class in the existing economic mode of production. He upheld his own theory as inescapable truth of the last oppressed class, which brings to an end the dialectical history of philosophies and of the ideologies they mask (Lavine, 1984).

Sartre did not take any of the extreme sides of the two finalities of Hegel and Marx on dialectical culminations. He synthesized the two to a modest position that for any society, at a particular time, there can be only one philosophy which can be fully expressive of it, and in this sense inescapable; this became his subject of human existence or existentialism.

Conclusion

In ancient Greece, dialectic as we have seen first dealt with cosmological questions, a reflection of the universe, then it developed to a form of reasoning that proceeded by question and answer as pursued by Socrates and Plato. In later antiquity and in the middle ages, the term was often used to mean simply logic and dialectic debate was guided by logical reasoning. Kant applied it to the arguments showing that principles of Science have contradictory aspects. Hegel in his political dialectic theory thought that all logic and world history followed dialectical path in which internal contradictions were transcended, but gave rise to new contradictions that themselves required resolution. Hegel as an idealist maintained that the highest state of man can only be attained through constant ideological conflict and resolution. He believed every historical revolution has been as a result of conflict and resolution. He taught in his dialectic theory that conflict takes man to the next spiritual level (Morgan, 2005). By taking this position, Hegel is seen to be justifying conflicts and endless wars in his ideology of endless movement from thesis- antithesis-synthesis. Karl Marx gave Hegel's idea of dialectic a material basis leading to dialectical materialism. Marx points out that Hegelian dialectic process is a tool for effecting change in which a concept or its realization passes over into, and is preserved and fulfilled by its opposite in development through the stages of thesis-antithesis-synthesis in accordance with the laws of dialectical materialism. William Shirer gave Hegel's dialectic theory a political perspective. According to Shirer's theory, one type of government or society (thesis) would give rise to another that was the opposite of this type of government or society (antithesis). This would result into conflict between the two types because they are opposites. After thesis and antithesis battle each other for some time without either winning, both sides become ready for change. This change (synthesis) is brought about by the creation of a third type of government or society (Shirer, 1959). The tensions give rise to new contradictions that evaporate leaving in their place a social world conceived in a new way as a collection of free and equal individuals subject to authority of law. According to the Hegelians, this triadic process could be what necessitated the birth of democratic concept, which is the subject of discussion in the next chapter.

CHAPTER 3

Evolution of Democractic Concept in Philosophical Cycles

Introduction

Although Philosophy is sometimes represented as a purely theoretical subject, concerned with abstract contemplation, philosophers have from earliest times seen it as part of their task to discover how human beings can live together, be fulfilled and happy in their society. This has evolved Philosophy from being viewed as abstract to being viewed as part of the social sciences touching on human existence in the empirical world. It therefore deals with man in his cultural context. All of us acquire directly or indirectly from our parents and teachers the social practices and certain guidelines on how to live, which form our culture in which we grow up. True to its characteristically critical function, philosophy never rests content with an acceptance of prevailing norms; it seeks to scrutinize those norms, to examine whether they are consistent and see how far they can be rationally justified (Cottingham, 2008).

Philosophers from the ancient to the contemporary period have wrestled with the rational explanation of concepts and ideas, their ultimate source and meaning as well as their objectively defensible standards. It is from such concern to address the fundamental issues of human existence that the discussion on democratic concept arose within the philosophical cycles as early as ancient period and has continued to evolve through the contemporary period.

The ideas presented in this part of the book cover some of the principal landmark philosophers on their political thought in the evolvement of democratic concept in the history of philosophy.

Philosophical and historical basis of Democratic concept

Sustained and sophisticated reflection on social, economic and political problems stretches back to the Ancient time, through the French revolution, when on the night of August 4, 1789, the National Assembly abolished the existing order to the present age (Kohler, 2014). The French revolution marked the moment when a judicial and social order forged over centuries, composed of hierarchy of separate orders, corps and communities; and defined by privileges, somehow evaporated. This collapse left in place a social world conceived in a new way as collection of free and equal individuals subject to the authority of law. The prior and present events and decisions have amounted to the philosophy's destruction of the world through dialectical evolvement from one era to another (Thomas, 2014). This has created a modern, individualistic society and posed a major problem; just how would these free, sovereign, equal and wholly autonomous individuals be related to, and united with one another? This has become the heart of what has come to be known as the social-political question; which raises the fundamental questions about human nature and the possibilities for pursuing life in common. A question that calls for one to address political, economic and legal relationships; that is, the nature of the family, work and other social relationships such as, the role of the state, the institutions of civil society, as well as the anthropology of the person.

Philosophers such as Karl Marx, John Stuart Mill, Edmund Burke, Alexis de Tocqueville, Herbert Spencer, Max Weber and John Paul II, as well as other thinkers have all addressed this social political question about autonomy or freedom in one form or the other. This question largely defined nineteenth and twentieth century politics, with communism and nationalism fronting two of the most powerful and opposing ideological answers (First things First, November 2014). Democratic ideologists claim to show the synthesis to the two opposing ideologies seen as thesis and antithesis. Perhaps, more than any other issue, this question of how to relate and unite the free, sovereign, equal and wholly autonomous individuals with each other remains one of the most pressing issues of our day. Democratic concept, among many other factors, has grown from the struggle to address this question.

Democracy: Philosophical and Conceptual meaning

The etymological meaning of the word democracy is the fifth century Greek word 'demokratia' which simply means rule by the people. This implies a form of regime whose legitimacy derives from the principle of popular sovereignty; namely, that, ordinary citizens are equally endowed with the right and ability to govern themselves (Guttmann, 1993). In contemporary practice, democracy is generally understood as government system whereby the governed people through their representative institutions, to which representatives are elected members through voting, for a period of time, exercise political power. The term democracy in this context stands for a political system of which it can be said that the whole people, positively or negatively make, and are entitled to make the basic determining decisions on important matters touching on public policy (Holden, 1974)

There are varying definitions of the term democracy. For instance, Flor McCarthy discusses democracy in terms of love and states that 'democratic love' is based upon equality under law. That is, we respect others because they are fellow citizens. We recognize their liberties in order that ours, in turn may be recognized and the reason for contributing to the good of others is the expectation of a return good (MacCarthy, 2000) However, there seem to be a generally conventional understanding in political field that democracy is a distinctive set of political institutions and practices, a particular set of rights, a social and economic order, a system that ensures desirable results or a unique process of making collective and binding decisions. It also involves the electoral procedures for choosing political elites to dispense expansive visions of citizen participation in political parties, groups, and work-place organization. This is the meaning of modern democracy, which has come to be applied to "representative democracy". Undoubtedly, the increased size of post-colonial political citizenry or community and the wide range of development issues have inexorably encouraged representative forms of governance in many regions of the world.

Democratic concept: Its evolution in the history of Philosophy

Ancient Greek to Modern Period

The term democracy first appeared in philosophical writings early fifth century. Its early practice and development can be traced in the Ancient Greek states like Athens where the Sophists and Socrates had great philosophical influence. According to philosophical writings at this time, the concept democracy consistent not only the majority rule, but also the actual participation of the people themselves.

Plato

According to Plato (427-347 BC), democracy is dependent on the changeable opinions of the many rather than on the certain knowledge of the philosopher who through the study of dialectics has seen the forms, the true and unchanging nature of things (Coplestone, 1962). For him democracy comes about when the poor, who are the majority in the state, join forces to fight the rich and eventually win the war. The resulting government, by the masses is democracy. He illustrates this by stating;

"And I suppose that democracy comes about when the poor are victorious, killing some of their opponents and expelling others, and giving the rest an equal share in ruling under the constitution, and for the most part assigning people to positions of rule by lot" (Cooper, 1997)

Plato's ideal state as illustrated in his book "Republic" was to be ruled by a philosopher king, well trained in morals and administration. In his advocacy of the rule by philosopher kings, he showed his distaste of the rule by the people for the people which was widely seen as democracy and practiced in Athens at his time. However in his later writings, the Laws, he showed his taste for democracy, even advocating for some elements of democracy to be included in his blue print government and recommends constitutionalism and active participation of mature citizens in the daily running of the state affairs (Kraut, 1992).

Aristotle

Aristotle (384-332 BC) was a student of Plato. Aristotle disregarded democracy in favor of monarchy. He dismissed democracy as the best among the worst forms of government. He cautioned against the undesirable effects of the regimes that polarized the rich and the poor and identified democracy with immoderation, regarding it as a source of political instability and prudence in his politics. However, Aristotle in his work 'Polis', implicitly advocated for democratic phenomena, that is, the rule of law, virtue and good for all individuals or what he calls justice. But he also in contradiction to this hails slavery as a necessity for good life (Miller, 1987).

Aristotle, like his teacher Plato, argued for an analogically democratic government. They both underlined the need for a transparent system of government which has the tenets of justice, rule of law and also called for high and moral qualifications for those to be allowed to hold office.

St. Augustine and St. Thomas Aquinas

St. Augustine of Hippo (354- 430) and St. Thomas Aquinas (1225-1274) were philosophers of great influence in the scholastic period. Their doctrines on the concept of democracy complemented each other. St. Augustine wrote on "An ideal State" in his work, the 'City of God'. He upheld Plato and Aristotle's inclusion of virtue and the rule of law in the art of government. For him the individual with respect to his freedom is presented before the others as a moral absolute. His notion of freedom is that it is inviolable and has to be upheld and promoted by the state and the other individuals. St. Thomas adopted Aristotle's concept of justice, for him the just is related to particular conception of the good of man. His democratic concept is seen in his concept of freedom of man. For him, without freedom there is no justice; What he called the *'conditio sine quo non'* for the good of man is freedom. He upheld Augustinian definition of justice as a multitude tied together on the basis of a juridical agreement. In his implicitly democratic concept, he manifests his sympathy for the form of government that favors more the political self-determination of the citizens. According to St. Thomas, freedom being the *conditio sine quo non,* for the good of man has to be regulated by an objective moral instance that determines which freedom is right and which freedom is wrong. For him, this moral instance is the natural law, and it demands respect for those with whom you live (Aquinas Thomas, Summa Contra Gentiles III, ch.112, 1).

Niccolo Machiavelli

Niccolo Machiavelli (1469-1527) was an Italian political theorist of the renaissance period. He wrote three great works on politics and governance, The Prince, the Discourses, and the Art of War. He redefined politics as an autonomous activity leading to the creation of free and powerful States. He never openly advocated for democracy, though today his principles are occasionally used for tyrannical 'democracies'. He was much concerned with the acquisition, maintenance and protection of principalities. This led to his famous doctrine, 'the end justifies the means'. According to him, a political leader reserves the right to resort to evil when necessitated in order to achieve the end. With this turn into Machiavelli's politics, virtue becomes the ability to achieve effective truth regardless of any restraints at all whether moral, theological or philosophical. From the conventional perspective where democracy is seen as an institution of people's rights, freedom and justice, Machiavellianism in practice violates the very essential tenets of democracy, however, it has been described as a kind of democracy by some elites. Advocating his shrewd means to gain and retain power, Machiavelli demonstrated democracy as pure form of government that could be safely incorporated into Statecraft only as one component of mixed constitution (Davis, 1995). His main work "The Prince," is concerned with the discovery on how Principalities are won, how they are held, and how they are lost. He uses the example of the fifteenth century Italy and asserts that few rulers were legitimate; in many cases the rulers secured election by corrupt means. That is, the electorates were manipulated with intimidation or language as it happens with dialectic technique for political gain. His work, "The Prince," is very explicit in repudiating received morality where the conduct of rulers is concerned. Machiavelli says a ruler will perish if he is always good; he must be as cunning as a fox and as fierce as a lion. Machiavelli poses the question;

"In which way must Princes keep faith?" He says that they should keep faith when it pays to do so, but not otherwise. A Prince must on occasion be faithless. But it is necessary to be able to disguise this character well and to be a great feigner and dissembler; and men are so simple and so ready to obey present necessities, that one who deceives will always find those who allow themselves to be deceived. An example is Alexander VI, he did nothing else but deceives men, he thought of nothing else but deceives and found occasion

37

for it; no stronger oaths and no man observed them less; however, he always succeeded in his deceptions as he knew well this aspect of things. It is not necessary therefore for a Prince to have all the conventional virtues, but it is very necessary to seem to have them. Above all, a Prince should seem to be religious" (The Prince, Chap. XVIII).

Proceeding from this thesis, Machiavelli advances an antithesis; that it seems to be recognized that political liberty requires a certain kind of personal virtue in the citizens. He cites Germany as an example where probity and religion were still common and there were many republics. Therefore, he says that in general, in this case the people are wiser and more constant than Princes and he concludes that it is not without good reason that in such case it is said the voice of the people is the voice of God. As it were, a synthesis in this dialectical triad would be that there are certain political goods, of which three are especially important, that is; national independence, security, and a well- ordered constitution. The best constitution is one which apportions legal rights among Prince, nobles and people in proportion to their real power, because under such constitution successful revolutions are difficult and therefore stability is possible. But for considerations of stability, it would be wise to give more power to the people, and that is what democracy does. A further analysis of Machiavelli's thought in the light of Hegelian dialectics would shed more light to our age to better appreciate Machiavelli's contribution in politics of modern and contemporary time. That is, notable success of our time has been achieved by use of methods as basic as those employed in Renaissance Italy.

Thomas Hobbes

Thomas Hobbes (1558-1679) was an English political philosopher of the early modern period, born in Wiltshire and Educated at Oxford. He made his major political contribution through a theory of his account of the nature of sovereignty and the grounds of political authority. Through the theory, he postulated an early version of what came to be known as the 'social contract' theory of the relationship between citizens and the government.

For him, human beings used to exist in a 'state of nature' or in a state of war of all against all because each individual seeks self- preservation and acquisition of property. But men had to come together, enter into a contract and entrust their rights to one individual or a group of individuals to govern them in order to end or save themselves from the wars. Government exists merely to maintain order for physical security of its subjects. This is because it is difficult to conceptualize a common good that makes any sense apart from self-preservation.

While Athenians were concerned with people governing themselves for themselves, Hobbes makes a radical departure from this traditional conception of democracy. His concern is how people might be protected from themselves and from others. Democracy in this classic sense is the realization of human potentialities through active participation in governing, but in liberal democracy, it offers only protection. Whilst in the traditional form, democracy is active and positive, and it enables and empowers. Hobbes concept of democracy is that of a passive acceptance of immunity in which freedom prevails and protects the governing and the governed (Seymour, 1995).

With his concept of social contract, Hobbes formed a basis and precedent of a kind of democracy, that of power coming from the people, being handed over to their leaders, a kind that demonstrates an art of representation. By their concepts, Hobbes and Machiavelli have been credited with laying of foundation upon which modern Western and Easter democracy rests or have evolved over the years.

John Locke

John Locke (1632-1704) was born in Somerset and educated in Christ Church-Oxford and became one of the England greatest philosophers. Locke made influential contributions to political theory in his 'Two treatises of Government' which discusses the nature of civil society and the basis of governmental authority.

Like Thomas Hobbes, he believed humans in the state of nature as being perfectly free and equal and pre-eminently concerned with their self-preservation. However, Locke's *state of nature* differ from Hobbes' in that; Locke's state of nature is one of peace where men are governed by the Law of Nature, promulgated by God, and capable of being understood by humans through their reason. This law of nature upholds human rights and freedom too (Seymour, 1995). Natural rights are the rights which belong to human being by nature, resting not on custom or convention, but on self-evident principles or fundamental laws or reason

(Collins, 1992). These are rights that are supposedly universal in scope and binding in human behavior, much like the physical laws of nature. According to Locke, natural rights were those enjoyed by Pre-historic humans in their original state of nature before humans began forming complex societies (Locke, 1966). This was an idyllic world of freedom, equality and consideration of other people's rights. In other words, humans lived in a tranquil and pleasant world devoid of chaos or anarchy because equality, freedom and consideration of other people's rights prevailed according to Locke's perspective of human existence in pre-historic times when there were no complex societies. Locke argues that;

"The state of nature is governed by a law of nature, which humans can discover through reason and humans were naturally free, equal and independent" (Locke, 1966: 39).

This argument from Locke is in agreement with the Universal Declaration of Human Rights Charter as well as the creation of the democratic belief that all human beings are created equal by nature. Locke's belief in the state of nature meant that all human beings are equal in the sense that they have rights which are before those given to them by the society and cannot be taken away by the society. In developed democracies like United States of America, this doctrine has been upheld with the view that each person, regardless of his/her status in life, is to be accorded equal treatment before the law (Burton, 1985). However, in many other developing countries this doctrine has been continuously violated with impunity resulting to tensions and oppositions within and outside the government, this raises requirement for a more democratic approach to human rights.

Locke argues that through formation or entry into a contract, men can avoid the state of nature. They can do this by agreeing among themselves to enter into a contract in order to end the conditions experienced in the state of nature. Locke suggests this can be done in two stages:

(i) The people in a state of nature first contract among themselves to form a political society

(ii) They then contract to set up a government by surrendering their rights to one person or a group of people to enforce the law of nature, a function now performed solely by the government.

Locke advocated for a government formed by consent and on obligation of the rulers to the ruled. By so doing, he developed fundamental principles of liberal democracy that were influential in the history of democratic theory and practice. These principles include; natural liberty and equality of human beings, individuals' rights to life, property and liberty, government by consent, limited government, religious liberty, the rule of law, the separation of powers, the supremacy of society over government and the right of revolution (Plattner, 1995).

Locke is called the apostle of the 1688 revolution, the most moderate and successful of all revolutions. In his most celebrated work, "The Essay Concerning Human Understanding", Locke says that Empiricism and Idealism alike are faced with the problem to which so far philosophy has found no satisfactory solution. The problem is how to show we have knowledge of other things than our self and the operations of the mind. In his philosophy, Locke came to a conclusion that knowledge is the perception of the agreement or disagreement of two ideas. This would perhaps mean that when viewed from Hegelian dialectic, truth is a synthesis from the thesis and antithesis. Locke advances this argument in his work "Treatise on Government" where he begins by supposing what he calls a "state of nature" antecedent to all human governments. The difference between human laws as we find them in democratic governments and Locke's law of nature is that the law of nature consists of divine commands, and it is not imposed by any human legislature (Russel, 1972). The deficiency in Locke's law of nature is that it is not clear how real the state of nature is, or it is just Locke's mere illustrative hypothesis, neither is it clear how far he supposes it to have had historical existence. What Locke had to say about the state of nature and the law of nature is, but a repetition of the medieval scholastic doctrine of Saint Thomas Aquinas. Saint Thomas says that every law framed by man bears the character of a law exactly to that extent to which it is derived from the law of nature. But if at any point it is in conflict with the law of nature, it at once ceases to be a law; it is a mere perversion of the law (Russel, 1972). This is also the case in democratic societies where any law which is at any point in conflict with the constitution is regarded to be a bad law, a perversion of the law and should not be obeyed.

Jean-Jacques Rousseau

Jean-Jacques Rousseau (1712-1778) was born in Geneva. In his work, The Social Contract (Du Contrat Social), he argued that the source of political legitimacy was a voluntary subjection of each individual to the 'general will'. Also, in his work 'Emile' a philosophical novel, which he terms as an ideal educational resource, he argued that the naturally good and noble individual can develop freely into a social being through guidance and encouragement rather than coercion and restraint (Cottingham, 2008).

Rousseau shared Hobbes and Locke's realistic and activist orientation towards politics, their empiricist theory of knowledge, egoistic psychology, and rights based individualism, as well as their contract theory of state. However, he went further and derived a radical (seemingly contradictory) set of prescriptions that pointed simultaneously toward a highly collectivized, militantly patriotic and rigidly democratic republic. He leaned toward a hyper individualistic life of withdrawal from society and communion with nature and one's inner self. He was therefore a proponent of both extreme individualism, and extreme collectivism (Seymour, 1995).

Immanuel Kant

Immanuel Kant (1724-1804), wrote on democracy in his work, "Perpetual Peace" where he argues for democracy in domestic government and sees democratic government as a way to avoid international war. According to Kant, the process of democracy would produce rational decision- making that would serve the true interests of the majority of the people. He also effected the turn toward internationalizing the concept of human rights.

Kant effected a far-reaching transformation in the qualitative understanding of human rights. In his thought, human freedom is no longer understood primarily as a means for achieving the ends of self-preservation or the pursuit of happiness. It is from this understanding that he developed his moral principle which he called "categorical imperative". Building on the distinction introduced by Jean-Jacques Rousseau between natural liberty which consists in following one's own inclination, and civil or moral liberty which consists in self-imposed obedience to law, Kant identifies freedom with self-legislation. He extends Rousseau's notion of the 'general will', which constitutes the self-legislation of a particular political community, into a principle of universal human morality.

The central principle of that morality, which Kant called the 'Categorical Imperative', commands that human beings act only in accordance with maxims that they can also will to be universal laws. This means that we ought to treat humans always as ends and never only as means. This also implies there ought to be no violation of the rights of the other or of others. This is a fundamental tenet or characteristic of the concept of democracy. Kant therefore upheld and championed the inclusion of human rights and universal suffrage in democratic governance. By his moral principle or "Categorical Imperative" Kant advocated for the role of morality in democratic practice.

Jean-Paul Sartre

Jean-Paul Sartre (1905-1980) was a French philosopher whose ideas had great influence on the twentieth- century culture. Although Sartre did not write explicitly in his works on democracy per se, his existentialist outlook which emphasized the inescapable anguish of human existence in which we are condemned to be free implicitly points to democratic concept. In his existentialism, he examined the nature of human self- consciousness and the relationship between the self and others. He develops the concept of "bad faith"- which implies series maneuvers by which individuals attempt to escape their total responsibility for their lives. In his critique of dialectical reason, Sartre examined the Marxist view of society which criticized some democratic practices like capitalism.

Sartre accentuated the expression of existential freedom by all human beings. His liberal concept was very influential essentially in forming the foundation on which democratic ideals could stand. He has been credited with forming the ground on which American pragmatism, which is a constituent foundational principle of democracy and political system of the United States of America.

John Stuart Mill

John Stuart Mill (1806-1873), born in London, was one of the greatest British philosopher of the nineteenth Century. He was a champion of liberalism where he advances the thesis that the only justification for interfering with individual liberty is to prevent the harm of others. This was a great contribution to the democratic concept where individual rights and freedom are cherished, but to the extent that they do not interfere with the rights and freedom of others. Mill, unlike Jean-Paul Sartre, advocated for utilitarian ethical theory which underscores the quality and quantity of happiness for the majority. This led him to uphold the majority rule.

Friedrich Nietzsche

Friedrich Nietzsche (1844-1900), born in Saxony, was a passionate rhetorical critic of traditional ethics, religion and metaphysics. He wrote on declarations on human condition and how it may be 'overcome'.

Nietzsche does not appreciate democracy as such, he posits that aristocratic nature is to some degree bred into us, so that some of us are simply born better off than others, and that society as a whole thrives with strong aristocratic class. However, Nietzsche maintains that change is a predominant feature in reality. According to him, everything is always changing, thus ideas, wills and truth are constantly changing and points out that we are constantly competing for dominance. Whatever we see as "true" at a given moment is not objectively so but rather represents the victory of a particular will against the others working within us. Nietzsche's problem with objectivity given to democracy is that those who praise it are guilty in one way or another of denying or avoiding the fact that reality is composed of a constantly shifting competition between wills. They wish to see the universe as fixed, whether by divine law or the laws of nature, and wish to slacken the struggle and competition that characterize existence. He perceives any effort to resist struggle and change as contrary to life (Nietzsche, 1887). Nietzsche's views degraded democracy and praised strife and violence. He departed from the views of Locke, Hobbes and Rousseau who argued for democracy from St. Thomas Aquinas concept of natural law. Nietzsche's arguments for democracy with an analogy of constant change, concurs with Hegel's idea of all reality being in a constant dialectical movement.

John Dewey

John Dewey (1859-1952) was one of the great advocates of the pragmatist theory in America, a moral and political thought he co-shared with Charles Sanders Peirce (1839-1914) and William James (1842-1910). From a pragmatist perspective, ideas are true if they work, that is; if the idea forms part of people's experience in a way that satisfies them, then that idea is true. The pragmatic theory interprets each concept by tracing its respective consequences.

Dewey enunciated the need for the merger of education and democracy. He applied pragmatic theory to democracy by emphasizing that education is crucial for a good democratic practice. He contended that pragmatic approaches to society's problems could improve everyone's participation in the expanding possibilities of culture. The pragmatic endeavor to improve education of all in a democratic society was the unifying theme in Dewey's philosophy of democracy. Dewey postulated that democracy's highest purpose is to provide the best possible education for the citizens. It implies that, genuine democracy depends on the education of citizens, especially on their liberties, rights and justice.

Dewey also brought into democratic concept the notion of natural science and stated that democratic education should model itself on experimental natural sciences. He argued that democratic societies should seek insights from methods of natural science to learn how to deal with the challenges associated with democratic systems. However, according to him the two, democracy and natural science should play complementary roles as science needs the guidance of democratic moral values as well. It is likely that scientific researchers and politicians who have genuine democratic traits will portray in their work moral tenets such as; honesty, fairness, sincerity, acceptance for dialogue and open mindedness in issues of consensus building or during dialectical tensions. Pragmatic approach encourages people to remain open to review of challenges to their fundamental concepts in economics, politics as well as moral convictions. Democratic concept is strengthened by pragmatism in its promotion and championing of changeability, innovation, adaptability, progressiveness and opposition to blind faith and rigid complacency (Seymour, 1995). These are characteristics of Hegelian dialectic or triadic movements through thesis-antithesis- synthesis, a movement towards the absolute as Hegel calls it in his dialectic theory. These principles of, adaptability, progressiveness, open mindedness, consensus building, opposition and counter position, are the tenets upon which genuine democratic concept rests.

In liberal perspective, these traits in a democratic concept nurture transparency, checks and balances, and advocate for education and innovation from the citizens.

Hegel

Hegel, though did not address democracy directly in his dialectic debate, built indirectly in his political thought from the French revolution. The French revolution, which has become the supreme example of revolution in the modern world, is seen to be riddled with paradoxes. Its guiding philosophy is the enlightenment philosophy of reason, of the rational order and harmony of nature and human nature. However, its unintended outcome is a reversal, the opposite of reason, the reign of terror and its irrational passions and mob violence (Lavine, 1984). Its political goals were to overthrow the regime of Louis XVI and replace it with a republic. But the revolution ended with unintended consequence of the rise of Napoleon to power as the Emperor of France, whose iron rule was far more efficient absolutism than that of the executed king. The French revolution stands out as an example of the human struggle for freedom just as democratic concept is also seen by many philosophers as a struggle for human freedom and existence. However, Hegel in his dialectic concept argues that opposition in a evolutionally struggle can also depict a shameful human capacity for being swept up into self-righteous mob frenzy. Hegel developed his philosophic democratic concept as a juxtaposition of the reversals, ironies and paradoxes composing the opposition to absolutism and revolutionaries.

Hegel respected the form of Plato's theory of state much more than he did that of his early modern predecessors such as Locke, Hobbes and Rousseau. He argued that Locke, Hobbes and Rousseau perceived an individual from his or her natural needs, desires and freedom. For Hegel, this was a contradiction since nature and the individual are contradictory, the individual and the individual freedoms that define individuality as such, are late comers in human history. The problem with Locke, Hobbes and Rousseau according to Hegel is that they projected man as an individual, abstracted from modern society into a state of nature. On the other hand, Plato, according to Hegel, had grasped the idea of modern freedom; that is a free choice of the class to which one belongs, what property to possess, or, which career to follow (Allen, 2006). These are the ideals which were to become the basis of democratic practice.

Karl Popper

Karl Popper defined democracy in contrast to dictatorship or tyranny. For him, the definition of democratic practice should be focused on opportunities for the people to control their leaders and to oust them without need for a revolution. As such, for Popper, democracy has turned out to be the popular form of government in the absence of other better options. However, in its pragmatic meaning, the democratic concept continues to evolve dialectically to its different forms. In his political philosophy, Popper argued that State is a necessary evil, its powers are not to be multiplied beyond what is necessary. In this argument, he followed the principle of Ockham's razor, that entities or essences must not be multiplied beyond what is necessary. This is one of the factors in the dialectical development of democratic concept; that is, mutilating it to such an extent that it loses the meaning, which causes opposition leading to a different form in an endless triad.

According to Popper, if the State is to fulfill its function, it must have more power at any given rate than any single private citizen or public corporation. Although we might design institutions to minimize the danger that these powers will be misused, we can never eliminate the danger completely. This assertion by Popper points to the conclusion that, even in a democratic State, people will always have to pay for the protection of the State. Not only in the form of taxes, but even in the form of humiliation suffered, for example, at the hands of bullying government officials. They only should seek ways to avoid paying too heavily for it. In this case, the difference between a democracy and a tyranny is that under democracy the government can be got rid of without bloodshed, while under tyranny it cannot. Democracy as such cannot confer many benefits upon the citizen; neither should it be expected to do so. It provides no more than a framework within which the citizens may act in a more or less organized and coherent way (Popper, 1963). In this state of affairs, the democratic concept and its practice in democratic governments will keep on reflecting the Hegelian thesis, antithesis, synthesis evolvement in its historical development.

CHAPTER 4

The Dialectical Evolvement of Forms of Government

In the context of Hegel's dialectic concept, the discussion on the evolvement of democratic concept can be understood from a view of four regimes that have evolved over time, and tend to degrade successively to each other. These are: Timocracy, oligarchy, democracy, and tyranny.

Timocracy: Socrates defines a timocracy as a government of people who love rule and honour. He argues that timocracy emerges from aristocracy due to civil war breaking out among the ruling class and the majority. Socrates asserts that in this evolvement, over time many births occur of people who lack aristocratic qualities, slowly drawing people away from knowledge and education, toward money-making and the acquisition of possessions. This leads to a civil war between those who value wisdom and those who value material acquisition, the two will struggle until a just medium is compromised. The timocrats value war in so far as it satisfies a love of victory and honour. The timocratic

53

man loves physical training and hunting, and his abilities in warfare (Socrates, Book VIII).

Oligarchy: Temptations create confusion between economic status and honour which is responsible for the emergence of oligarchy. The injustice of economic disparity divides the rich and the poor, thus creating an environment for criminals and beggars to emerge. The rich are constantly plotting against the poor and vice versa. The oligarchic constitution is based on property assessment and wealth qualification. Unlike the timocrats, oligarchs are unwilling to fight or get into war since they do not wish to harm the majority for fear of their rising up against them, nor do they wish to pay mercenaries to fight for them since they are reluctant to spend their money. The prevailing disparity creates tension which escalates to a point where it becomes necessary to have a mediator or reach to a consensus (Socrates, Book VIII).

Democracy: As this socio-economic divide grows, so do the tensions between social classes. From the conflicts arising out of such tensions, the poor majority overthrows the wealthy minority, and democracy replaces the oligarchy preceding it. The poor overthrow the oligarchs and grant liberties and freedoms to citizens, creating a most variated collection of peoples under a constitution. In this view, a constitution is a visually appealing demagogue lifted up to protect the interests of the lower class. However, with too much freedom, no requirements for anyone to rule and having no interest in assessing the background of their rulers, other than honouring such people because they wish the majority well, people become easily persuaded by such demagogue's appeal to try and satisfy their common base, and unnecessary pleasures. This creates another tension which calls for a medium.

Tyranny: The excessive freedoms granted to the citizens of a democracy ultimately leads to a tyranny, the furthest regressed type of government. The freedoms provided by democracy divide people into three socio-economic classes: the dominating class, the elites and the commoners. Tensions between the dominating class and the elites cause the commoners to seek out protection of their democratic liberties. They invest all their power in their democratic demagogue, who, in turn, becomes corrupted by the power and becomes a tyranny with a small entourage of his supporters for protection and control of his people.

As observed in this evolvement from one form of government to another the process is always towards becoming what people or systems are capable of becoming, a self-actualization process as Stevenson Lewis calls it (Lewis, 1952). Hegel called it a triadic movement or dialectic process towards the absolute.

Dialectic debate and evolution of democratic concept

In a dialectic debate, social conversations are shifted, for example; a debate over market freedom versus socialism, to a debate about the degree of socialism that is desirable. Or, a debate over communism versus socialist democratic rule, to a debate about the degree of democracy that is desirable to a particular society in a given situation. In principle, one needs to emphasize one argument at the expense of the other, effectively shifting the political paradigm through a dialectical formula of triadic movement of thesis-antithesis-synthesis. This is a process of change in which a concept or its realization passes over and is preserved and fulfilled in its opposite. The development occurs through three stages; that is; thesis, antithesis and synthesis in accordance with the laws of dialectic materialism, systematic reasoning, exposition or argument that juxtaposes opposite/contradictory ideas and usually seeks to resolve their conflict (Merriam-Webster Dictionary). The concept applies to any dialectical tension between two interacting forces or elements.

Hegel pointed out that when we remain locked into dialectical thinking, we cannot see out of the dialectic box (Hegel, 1558). Its only when we step out of the dialectic box that we can be released from the limitations of controlled and guided thought. By so doing we will stop the privacy invasions, expanding police powers, and outright assault on individual liberty which overshadow the democratic process. Those who support capitalism stand against those who support socialism. The Hegelian dialectic, weaved in triadic movement from thesis to antithesis to synthesis guides the debate on democratization from the status quo to the desired democratic status through democratic means as well as other processes. As Hegel asserts, dialogue and consensus building are primary tools for the dialectic, but terror and intimidation can also be used as tools for obtaining the goal (Hegel, 1558).

Democratization Process as a Dialectical formula

The main discussion in this chapter has been on the evolvement of the democratic concept in the philosophical circles. The concept, democracy, is conventionally understood as a political system across countries where it shares similarities and demonstrates differences. In the same way, as demonstrated in this chapter, explaining the rhythm and reason of the democratic characteristics, similarities and differences in the thought and concept of this system, has intrigued a long line of philosophers. It began with Early Philosophers; the Sophists, Socrates, Plato, Machiavelli, Jean-Jacques Rousseau, John Stuart Mill, Hegel, down to present day thinkers and academicians.

Although these thinkers span time and place, each has approached from his or her perspective the enduring question of: How a society should balance individual rights versus the needs of the community to develop a rational, righteous, and harmonious system. How a society can guarantee individual freedom in the pursuit of economic self-interest. Whether a society should champion equality or accept hierarchy. As well as whether individual rights are inalienable or conferred by a collective bargain through entering into a social contract by the ruled with the rulers.

Engaging into these pertinent questions evolved to democratic political thought as a way of uniting a society in the face of divisive viewpoints. This development has not been linear; rather, as evidenced by arguments and counter arguments from different philosophers, it has gone through a dialectical movement resembling thesis-antithesis-synthesis.

Some philosophers have embraced individualism- a doctrine that champions the primacy of individual freedom, self-expression, and independence. Others have underscored collectivism, a doctrine that advocates for the primacy of the rights and role of the group. One group would play the thesis while the other would play the antithesis in this scenario.

We deduce from the discussion here that, translating the implications of individualism and collectivism to a political system evolved to the construction of democracy as a political ideology. In theory, an ideology is an integrated vision that defines a holistic conception of an abstract ideal and its normative thought process (Sullivan, 2011). For example, the ideal democracy carries with it several philosophical presumptions about corollary principles, doctrines, goals, practices, and symbols.

As Lewis Stevenson observed, we are in the process of becoming all that we are capable of becoming (Lewis, 1952), a process metaphysics would call self-actualization. This is the case with democratic concept; it has always been in the process of evolvement through dialectical movement in its history and in the minds of philosophers.

The evolvement of democratic concept in philosophical cycles has mainly been dominated by two philosophical groups: the idealists-those who prefer to establish overall principles before they try to resolve small issues, or tend to focus on the whole then on the parts. On the other hand are the pragmatists-those who prefer to focus more on details than on abstract principles or first to focus on the parts then on the whole. Each of the group has approached the concept from its perspective. This portrays the characteristics of dialectic concept in the context of dialectical development of democratic systems.

The fundamental element of democracy is freedom, whether freedom of speech, freedom of association, freedom of belief, or freedom in any other part of life. A number of political ideologies in practice today champion different standards of political freedom. For instance, classical liberal philosophy holds that freedom is the absence of coercion of one man by his fellow man. Jurisprudence holds that an individual has the right to determine one's own actions autonomously. Environmentalism advocates constraints on the use of ecosystems in any definition of freedom. Others take a more abstract approach discussing notions of positive freedom versus negative freedom with those on the positive referring to the right to fulfill one's own potential as fundamental freedom, and the negative referring to the freedom from restraints as fundamental tenet. For example, former British Prime Minister Winston Churchill noted that democracy is the worst form of government except all those other forms that have been tried from time to time (The Economist, July 17, 1999).

Therefore, although seen as superior to its alternatives democracy still exhibits imperfections which make its dialectical evolvement continuous through position and counter position. This movement is synonymous to what Hegel calls a movement towards the absolute through thesis, antithesis, synthesis. For instance, some fledgling democracies that emerged in the past decades, especially those in the former Soviet bloc countries are still struggling with domestic unrest and security threats. These events result to restrictions on freedoms and raise questions about the legitimacy of democracy necessitating a movement from the status quo. Additionally, the global economic crisis which threatens the rise of middle class propels the evolvement of democracy. History shows that right-wing conservative movements generally draw their popular support from middle classes seeking to preserve the status quo. Furthermore, people falling back into poverty are politically hazardous. Left-wing progressives have often developed from working class movements seeking to overthrow perceived oppressors. Consequently, the growing risk of a shrinking middle class in the face of the economic and political instability due to global economic crisis, threaten to undo the democratic progress in developing countries (The Economist, March 14, 2009). This keeps the democratization process dialectically evolving.

From a conventional perspective, democracy has been understood to stand for "a government of the people, by the people, and for the people". This implies that the people participate in decision making. However, the population of most nations makes participation by all voters in the democratic process impossible. Therefore, throughout history many democratic countries have seen the practice of their democracy evolve into various forms (Sullivan et al, 2011). In systematic or in other cases very disruptive ways, democracy dialectically evolves into the following types:

Parliamentary Democracy: For this type of democracy, the citizens exercise political power by electing representatives to a legislative branch of government called a parliament. The executive branch typically consists of a cabinet headed by a prime minister or a president who is regarded as head of the government. There is independent judiciary but no formal separation of powers between the executive and legislative branches. Examples of these include Australia and India. Dissatisfied citizenry cause political disruption in this form of democracy to move from the status quo to liberal democracy.

Liberal Democracy: This form of democracy originates in a constitution that protects certain individual freedoms such as; freedom of speech, freedom of assembly and freedom of religion, as well as certain individual liberties such as the right to property and privacy. All citizens, both public and private are presumably treated equally before the law and receive due process under the law. Japan and New Zealand are examples of this form of democracy. Despite the presumed equality under the law, some groups from either political or economic class cause disruption which necessitates an evolvement to another form known as multiparty democracy.

Multiparty Democracy: This type of democracy defines a political system whereby three or more political parties, whether separately or as part of a coalition govern. The multiparty system prevents the leadership of a single party from setting policy without negotiating compromises among the opposition parties. Canada, Germany, Italy, and Israel are examples of this democracy. Not all parties are comfortable for long with this governing system, therefore counter positions challenge the status quo leading to another form of democracy called representative democracy.

Representative Democracy: A representative democracy is one in which the people's elected representatives hold ultimate sovereignty. Representatives are charged with the responsibility of acting in people's interest and not merely as their proxy representatives. In other words, officials represent voters, and while mindful of voter preferences, they still command the authority to act as they deem fit. United States is an example of this type of democracy. The electorate who vote in or out the representatives are presumed to be involved in decision making through their representatives, however as in multiparty democracy, this system involves either two or more parties who are many times in opposition to each other, therefore, with time this form shows imperfections challenging the status quo. This leads to a movement towards another type of democracy known as social democracy.

Social Democracy: This type of democracy advocates the use of democratic means to achieve a gradual transition from capitalism to socialism. This view of democracy rests on the belief that society must regulate and reform capitalism to control its intrinsic tendency toward justice and opportunism. The term social democracy is largely interchangeable with democratic socialism. Examples of this form of democracy are Norway and Sweden.

The dialectical movement of democratic concept does not end with any given type of democracy. As illustrated earlier in the last chapter, this movement continues to run throughout history, weaved in a dialectical formula as; thesis (democracy)-antithesis (social democracy)-synthesis (the degree of socialism that is desirable).

Political systems across countries share similarities and demonstrate differences. Explaining the rhythm and reason of these characteristics has intrigued a long line of philosophers, beginning with Plato and Confucius, and moving on to touch such thinkers as Machiavelli, Adam Smith, Jean-Jacques Rousseau, John Stuart Mill and Milton Friedman. Although they span time and place, each has wrestled with same enduring questions: How should society balance individual rights versus the needs of the community to develop a rational, righteous, and harmonious system? Should society guarantee individual freedom in the pursuit of economic self-interest? Does society fare better when individual rights are subordinated to collective goals? Should society champion equality or accept hierarchy? Are individual rights inalienable or conferred by the collective? Engaging these questions by philosophers and other cadre of thinkers anchors interpretation of the political systems in terms of individualism (as thesis) versus collectivism (as antithesis).

Individualism

Individualism refers to the primacy of the rights and role of the individual. It is a doctrine that emphasizes the primacy of individual freedom, self-expression, and personal independence: "the principle that all human beings have certain unalienable rights; that among these are life, Liberty and pursuit of happiness" (Sullivan et al, 2011: 93).

Individualism champions the exercise of one's ambitions and desires, while opposing most of the external interference posed by the political system that constrain individual choice. Furthermore, individualism presumes that the task of the political system is to develop a form of government that protects the liberty of individuals to act as they wish, as long as their actions do not infringe on the liberties of others.

For instance, the business implications of individualism hold that each person commands the right to make economic decisions largely free of rules and regulations. Countries with an individualist orientation shape their marketplace with the ideology of laissez-faire. The ideology laissez-faire literally means "leave things alone". In the business realm, it holds that government should not interfere in business affairs. Instead, agents behave and the market operates according to the neo-liberal principles of market fundamentalism. Individuals are presumed to be self-regulating in promoting economic prosperity and growth, acting fairly and justly to maximize personal performance without threatening the welfare of society (Sullivan et al, 2011). Countries with individualistic orientation include the United States, Australia, the United Kingdom, Canada, Netherlands and New Zealand. Gaps between philosophical ideals and opportunistic behaviors often fan an adversarial relationship between governments and certain cadre of individuals in individualistic societies leading to a counter position known as collectivism.

Collectivism

Collectivism refers to the primacy of the rights and role of the group. It is a doctrine that emphasizes the primacy of the collective-whether it is a group, party, class, society, nation or race over the interest of the individual. It holds to the principle that the whole is greater than sum of the parts. That is, no matter the importance of the individuals that comprise the group, ultimately the group as a whole is greater than the sum of its parts. It endorses the priority of the goals of the group; individuals sometimes by birth, or sometimes by subsequent socialization, define their identity subsequently. Collectivism integrates individuals into cohesive societies that accept the principle that, as Ayn Rand noted, "Require self-sacrifice and the subordination of one's interests to those of others" (Sullivan et al, 2011). Countries with collectivistic orientation include Argentina, China, Vietnam, Japan, North Korea, Egypt, Brazil and Mexico.

For instance, collectivism in the business world holds that the ownership of assets, the structure of industries, the conduct of companies, and the actions of managers must improve the welfare of society. It is from this principle that even business corporations in individualistic countries have developed ethical and corporate social responsibility policies. In collectivism systems, business decisions are made by the group, and group members assume joint responsibility. Systems that feature a collectivist orientation hold that government intervenes in market situations to ensure that business practices benefit society. For example, in many cases, governments in collectivist societies such as Sweden take actions that promote social equality, labor rights, balanced income distribution, and workplace democracy. In extreme cases such as those of Venezuela or North Korea, political leaders may overrun personal privacy, control mass media and profess the ideologies of harmony, consensus, and equality in their efforts to control the economy. Despite the harmony presumed in the collectivist orientation, with time an adversity occurs in the group, an antithesis to the collectivism (thesis) which results to a counter position known as pluralism.

Pluralism

Pluralism, in principle holds the belief that there are multiple opinions about an issue, each of which contains part of the truth, but none that contain the entire truth. For example, in Japan and the United States, as in many other countries, there are other active political parties that list smaller memberships than the main factions. Consequently, most societies are pluralistic systems in which different groups champion competing political ideologies. Pluralism is not restricted to institutional demographics, it also arises when two or more groups in a country differ in terms of language, as in Belgium, class structure-as in the United Kingdom, ethnic background-as in South Africa, tribal legacy-as in Afghanistan, or religion-as in India. However, more common are pluralistic systems marked by a diversity of formal groups advocating competing political ideologies. Pluralism rests upon ideas drawn from the sociology of small groups. When translated to a level of a society, these ideas make sense of the relationships and interactions between and within groups as they champion and contest Political ideologies. In a pluralistic society, government does not command the authority to act unilaterally. Rather, government's task is to balance the initiatives championed by various groups. The fact that these groups anchor their agendas in different political ideologies calls upon the government to negotiate solutions. Consequently, ambiguity often marks decision making in pluralistic societies. The ambiguity calls for a resolution, which leads to development of higher form of political ideology.

This dialectical movement in a thesis, antithesis, and synthesis triad is endless as each stage is followed by an opposition leading to a new stage in a cycle of transitions.

Hegel postulated that dialogue and consensus building are primary tools of the dialectic, but terror and intimidation can also be acceptable formats for obtaining the goal, that is, to push for change from status quo

It was earlier noted how unsatisfied parties move democratic concept from one form to another. As logicians point out, in the use of the dialectic, to move the public from point A to point B, one need only to find a spokesperson as an authority or create a crisis for a certain argument and position the spokesperson as an authority. That person would represent Goal Post One. Another person is positioned on the other side of the argument to represent goal Post Two. Argument A and B can then be used to manipulate a given social discussion. For example; to promote idea C. In this case, one merely needs to promote the arguments of goal post One that tend to promote the idea C more effectively than the arguments of Goal Post Two. This forces a slippage of goal post Two's position. Thus, goal post one and Goal post Two advance downfield toward idea C. Eventually, goal post Two occupies goal post One's original position. The "anti-C" argument now occupies the "Pro-C" Position.

Since the time of John Locke, we have been duped to believe the State has supreme right against the individual, whose supreme duty is to be a member of the State; for the right of the world spirit is above all special privileges (Shirer, 1959). According to him, Hegelian principle defined a method used to produce oneness of mind on any given issue or thought. Since its conception, it has been used repeatedly and very successfully to gain power, status, money, and control. In his analysis of Hegel's theory from a political perspective, one type of government (Thesis) would give rise to another that is the opposite of the present type (antithesis). This would result into conflict between the two types since they are opposing each other. After thesis and antithesis ideas battle each other for an extended time without either side winning, both sides become ready for change. This change /synthesis is brought about by the creation of a third type of government. When the public is conditioned to ask for change democratization process evolves to a new stage.

CHAPTER 5

Conclusion

As noted earlier, Hegel asserted that dialectic is the synthesis of opposites, that is, every concept, as we think about it, begins to show us its limitations and passes over into its opposite, into the very negation of itself (Hegel, 1956). Understood in this context, the dialectic in the sense of Heraclitus concept of continuous change, opposition, conflict, polarity, or contradiction characterizes the democratization process. Just as the Heraclitus principle asserts, that change characterizes all human thought, our thoughts on democratic phenomenon are always evolving. Heraclitus had used an example of stepping in flowing water and asserted that "You cannot step in the same water twice".

However, early philosophers who studied Heraclitus dialectic asserted that his concept, once its reflected upon, begins to show limitations and it passes over into its opposite in Permenide's claim that nothing changes. This seems true of democracy at every stage or election; that is, once reflected upon, nothing changes in terms of the democratic principles. We find ourselves in what Heraclitus

69

and Permenides created, that is, two goal posts. Just as Hegel came to mediate upon Heraclitus and Permenides and called the concept of Heraclitus the thesis, and that of Permenides the antithesis, and he came to offer a synthesis, we always find this need after every other election for an ongoing need for mediation.

The democratization process supports Hegel's conclusion that each historical event represents not only change but progress; and one historical event or phase tends to be replaced by its opposite, which is later replaced by a resolution of the two extremes. He called this a third law of his dialectic. Scholars and students of history termed it the "pendulum theory", that is, events wing from one extreme to the other before the pendulum comes to rest at the middle. The extreme phases are called the thesis and the antithesis, the resolution is called the synthesis.

The democratization process illustrates Hegel's dialectic principle in theory and practice. However, from a pragmatic view of those who use it in politics, it is negated to manipulate the electorate to falsely believe that those agitating for change are doing it for their benefit. For instance, as pointed out earlier, democratic governments should represent people who are free from the imperial and tribal controls over private and national resources, trade and production. Democratic governments should protect their citizens from tribal slavery by protecting the resources and institutions through just laws, equal rights and obligations. However, Philip Worts points out that those in political power many times use the dialectic to manipulate the population in order to stay in power or gain more of it (Worts, 2012). He adds that dialectic is twisted logic used by political "cons" in such way to be hardly penetrable by electorate in the election campaigns. According to Worts, like Hegel and his followers the best political "con" knows his spiel has to use dialectic logic to bend and distort the story. Hence, many politicians as well as leaders of different cadres manipulate the public by weaving their lies on dialectical or mathematical progression. This makes it hard for ordinary citizens to note the fallacy which is in the language, not in the math (Worts, 2012).

The dialectical manipulation imposes limitations on the democratic practice and keeps the urge for ongoing democratization process at every stage. This can also be understood as the process of becoming from the metaphysics point of view on the concept of being and becoming. The cause of the continuous change is the search for fulfillment of the forces that dialectically propel the dialectical evolvement of democracy.

On the basis of historical development, the fall of the Berlin wall in 1989 and the ensuing collapse of the Communist Bloc led to the swelling of the third wave of democratization, which gave rise to the notion of the so – called "end of history". This notion held that the democratic ideology, reinforced by the market fundamentalism of capitalism represented the final stage of social development. Francis Fukuyama reflecting on this historical episode reasoned that,

"What we are witnessing is not just the end of the Cold War, or the passing of a particular period of post-war history, but the end of history as such: that is, the end of point of mankind's

71

ideological evolution and the universalization of Western liberal democracy as the final form of human government" (Fukuyama, 1992:42).

Fukuyama's perception was influenced by the match towards greater political freedoms and expansive civil liberties prevalent beginning in the 1970's fueled by the belief in the inevitability of democracy, the so called "end of history" phenomenon (Fukuyama, 1992). Since 1970's the wave of democratization has been worldwide with countries from Africa, Asia, Latin America, South America, and Eastern Europe emerging into, or advocating for democracies based on greater individual freedoms and expanded civil liberties. Societies began fighting for, or building fairer civic institutions, independent media, objective judiciaries, and stronger property rights (Fukuyama: 1992).

Despite the importance given to democratic concept and the struggle for democratization process, its practice has been challenged leading to continuous movement or development of the understanding and application of the concept. For instance, the legitimacy of Western notions of democracy, when applied to societies that do not have the same level of comfort with its ideals and institutions has come under question. Hu Jintao, China's president and Communist Party chief gave a different view of democracy from the one understood by Westerners. In his view, calls for multiparty democracy are a taboo, opposition cannot officially organize, reform must obey the "correct political orientation", and change must be in an "orderly" way that upholds the party's leadership (Economist, June 28, 2007: 44). Russian

72

Prime Minister, Vladimir Putin, proclaiming that "I am a true democrat", argues that his country's application of authoritarianism has been misinterpreted. He criticized the West charging that the "largest complexity today is that some of the participants in the international dialogue believe that their ideas of democracy are the ultimate truth (Spiegel, June 28, 2015).

Brazil's president Luiz Inacio Lula da Silva supported Putin's view by arguing that countries like the United States, United Kingdom, Germany, France, Canada and Japan, the primary advocates of Western style democracy no longer speak for the world. He contends that these countries have lost the moral authority to solve the world's problems and dictate solutions to poorer countries (The Telegraph, March 16, 2009: A-1).

Alternative points of perspective as antithesis to democracy have been raised, fortified by charges of hypocrisy against the United States. Owing to its incursion in Iraq and Afghanistan, along with the implications of its antiterrorist activities to political freedoms and civil liberties have raised an intricate question, namely; what constitutes democracy in action? Consequently, antithetical positions have been held questioning whether democracy, at least in the form advocated by the world's veteran democracies can consistently be the most preferred political system. Such positions and counter positions have led democracy to persist in the form of liberal democracy as in the United States, transmute into a single-party system like in China, as well as into a clash of civilizations giving rise to new ideas of freedom and liberty.

The political views and positions expressed above have propelled the dialectical movement of democracy into its evolvement throughout history. However, there are general factors that continue to power the wave of democratization in most parts of the world. Most notably, they include: Actions of aggrieved citizens who contest the right of political officials to govern. For example, the fall of the Berlin Wall punctuated this epic change. As formerly Communist countries adopted democratic principles and practices, they weakened the links between new political practices and economic habits (Sullivan et al, 2011). In addition, improved communications technology eroded totalitarian states' control of information. Democracy benefits from an informed public with easy access to media. Images of resistance and rebellion have great effect on the campaign for democratic reform. Today, expanding internet access engages previously disenfranchised people worldwide. Access to the world beyond the village, seen earlier perhaps only when newspapers arrived in a bundle only in the morning or when a neighbor returned from a trip in the city, reporting yesterday's happenings, is now available through expanding wireless and satellite systems. Plugged into the internet, more people are receiving news and processing information just in time. As Thomas Jefferson, author of the Declaration of Independence and third President of the United States observed "Information is the currency of democracy" (Freedom in the World, 2006).

The other factors that keep democratization process evolving in Hegelian triadic movement are the fundamental features of democratic political systems. These include: Freedom of opinion, expression, press, religion, association and access to information. Exercise of citizen power and civic responsibility, either directly or through elected representatives, and, citizens' equality in opportunity and treatment before the law plus free fair and regular elections. In addition, majority rule coupled with protection of individual and minority rights with fair and independent court system charged with protecting individual rights and property with subordination of the government to the rule of law has accelerated democratization process.

When one form of democracy starts to show a limitation to either one or some of these features, an opposition (antithesis) to the status quo (thesis) occurs, leading to a counter-position (synthesis). A study carried out and reported by Freedom House agency in their annual survey of political rights and civil liberties in 119 electoral democracies in the world in 1987 reflected this dialectical movement (Freedom in The World, 2008). Indications in the report showed a slowing adoption and growing skepticism of the conventional principles of democracy which are interpreted in the dialectic concept as a potential for Hegelian triadic thesis-antithesis -synthesis movement. A downward trend from the status quo of democratic form in a given country would signify a decline in democracy, or put differently, an antithesis in the triad (Freedom House, 2009).

Social advancement is the triadic blending of thesis, antithesis and synthesis. When a particular theory or thesis loses its competence and power to effect collective welfare, an antithesis is created against the prevalent theory. As a result of the clash and tension between these two opposing forces, a resultant is created and this resultant is called synthesis. However, the welfare is not is not yet fulfilled in the stage of the synthesis. Such a movement of the social cycle never ceases, it never stops. When those who have the duty and responsibility for materializing social welfare neglect minorities or the people in general, the synthesis of a particular age transforms itself into thesis of the next age. This movement can be understood from an empirical perspective or approach, everything in the empirical world has its roots in relativity; and everything is moving within the orbit of time, space and person.

In the stage of synthesis a particular social, economic and political theory may be beneficial in a particular place, or to a particular group, but this is not a guarantee that the same theory will prove equally beneficial with changes in time, space and person. In changed circumstances oppressed people, who pass their days in distraction and despair as victims of social injustice, put up an antithesis against the synthesis of that period. In democratic situations, numerical might or the tyranny of numbers matter where voting is the criteria for change. However, numerical might and physical might are not always or in all places and circumstances the sole prerequisites for the emergence of an antithesis. For example, if the oppressed are an intellectual group, then no matter how few their numbers, they can put up an antithesis. As soon as the antithesis is created, the former ideology ceases to be a synthesis. It becomes the thesis in the next phase. So, in the second phase, an antithesis will again emerge against that very thesis. In this phase, as long as a synthesis does not emerge, unabated struggle will continue. Theoretically, synthesis is not the absolute factor, the final clash or the last word, for thesis, antithesis and synthesis take place within the bounds of relativity.

In the dialectic perspective, democracy cannot absolutely fulfill the welfare or the human well-being of human society. One form at a particular time, place and people, it may be suitable and appropriate for the well-being of human society in that certain age, but in the very next era it may prove to be a brutal instrument of exploitation and destruction. The policies and programmes formulated for a particular era, for a particular place, and for particular people will not remain fixed in new conditions and will adjust with changes in time, space and person. Such are the principles under which democratic practice is built. An understanding of its historical development, the events of democratic struggle including violence, detentions, constitutional changes and consequent elections should take into account this dialectical perspective.

References

Ackermann, R. J. (1976). *The Philosophy of Karl Popper.* Massachusetts: University of Massachusetts Press.

Allen, R. (2006). *Plato: The Republic.* New Haven: Yale University Press.

Anyang Nyong'o, P. (1963). *Arms and Daggers in the Heart of Africa.* Nairobi: Academy of Sciences.

Aquinas, T. (n.d.). *Summa Contra Gentiles.*

Arend, t. H. (1965). *The Human Codition.* Chicago: University of Chicago Press.

Arieli, Y. (1964). *Individualism and Nationalism in American Ideology.* Massachusetts: Harvard University Press.

Aristotle. (1980). *Nichomachean Ethics.* Oxford: Clarendon Press.

Arnold I. Davidson, A. S. (1988). *Reconstructing Individualism: Anatomy, Individuality, and the Self in Western Thought*. Stanford: Stanford University Press.

Austin, J. L. (1965). *How To Do Things with Words*. New York: Oxford University Press.

Avineri, S. (1972). *Hegel's Theory of Modern State*. Cambridge: Cambridge University Press.

Ayer, A. J. (1946). *Language, Truth and Logic:*. New York: Dover.

Ball, T. (1980). *Utilitarianism, Feminism and the Franchise, James Mill and His Critics: A History of Political Thought*. London: Earthscan Publications.

Barry, B. (1989). *Theories of Justice: A Treatise on Social Justice, Vol. 1*. London: Harvester-Wheatsheaf.

Berlin, I. (1969). *Four Essays on Liberty*. Oxford and New York: University Press.

Berman, M. (2009). *The Politics of Authenticity: Radical Individualism and the Emergence of Modern Society*. London: Verso.

Block, M. (1983). *Marxism and Anthropology*. New York: Oxford University Press.

Bolton, F. P. (1948). *Communism, Its Plans and Tactics*. Washington DC: Infantry Journal Press.

Boralevi, L. (1969). *Bentham and the Oppressed.* Berlin: University Press.

Burke, T. E. (1983). *The Philosophy of Popper.* Manchester: Manchester University Press.

Burton, C. (1985). *Subordination: Feminism and Social Theory.* Hertfordshire: George Allen & Unwin Publishers.

Campell, T. (1998). *Justice.* London: Macmillan Education Ltd.

Cardinal, O. M. (1979). *Historical Society, Reprints, Vol.1.*

Cletus, C. (2002). *Introduction to Philosophy in an African Perspective.* Eldoret: Zapf Chancery.

Comet, A. (1975). *A General View of Positivism.* London: Robert Speller and Sons Publishers Ltd.

Cooper, J. M. (1997). *Plato: Complete Works.* Indiapolis: Hackett Publishing Company Inc.

Cottigham, J. (2008). *Western Philosophy: An Anthology (2nd ed).* Massechussites: Blackwell Publishing.

Cottingham, J. (1988). *Descartes: Principles.* Cambridge: Cambridge University Press.

Court, D. &. (1974). *Education, Society and Development: New perspectives from Kenya.* Oxford: Oxford University Press.

Crospey, L. S. (1987). *History of Political Philosophy (3rd ed.).* Chicago: The University of Chicago Press.

Curley, E. (1985). *Collected Works of Spinoza, Vol 1.* Princeton: Princeton University Press.

Daniels, R. &. (2011). *International Business: Envrionments and Operations.* New Jersey: Prentice Hall Inc.

David, K. (1990). *Demonstratives: Readings in Philosophy.* Oxford: Oxford University Press.

Donald, D. (1984). *Dialectica.* Cambridge: Sydney Shoemaker.

Edwards, P. (1967). *The Encyclopedia of Philosophy. Vol. 1-8.* New York: Macmillan.

Eisenstein, Z. R. (1979). *Capitalist Patriarchy and Case for Socialist Feminism.* New York: Monthly Review Press.

F., H. G. (1977). *Hegel's Phenomenology of Spirit (Trans. A. V. Miller).* Oxford: Oxford University Press.

Foster, M. B. (1935). *The Political Philosophies of Plato and Hegel.* Oxford: Oxford University Press.

Franz, W. (1968). *Hegel: An illustarted Biography*. New York: Pegasus.

Frye, M. (1983). *The Politics of Reality*. New York: The Crossing Press.

Fuer, L. S. (1959). *Karl Marx and Friedrich Engels: Basic Writings on Politics and Philosophy*. New York: Doubleday.

Georg, H. (1959). *The Rise and Fall of the Third Reich*. Oxford: Oxford University Press.

George, H. S. (2015). *Individualism*. Massachusetts: CATO Institute.

Guttiry, G. (2001). *French Philosophy in the Twentieth Century*. London: Cambridge University Press.

Guttman, A. (2014, November 11). Rebuilding Democracy. *First Things First*, pp. 3-8.

Guttman, A. (November, 2014). Democracy. *First Things First*, 12-15.

H., W. W. (1969). *Hegelian Ethics*. New York: St. Martin's Press.

Habermas, J. (1996). *Between Facts and Norms: Contributions to a Discourse theory of Law and Democracy*. Massachusisetts: MIT Press.

Harris, H. S. (1972). *Hegel's Development: Towards the Sunlight.* Oxford: Clarendon Press.

Harvey, M. (1998). *The Prince: Nicollo Machiavelli (2nd ed.).* Chicago: University of Chicago Press.

Hegel, F. J. (1958). *A Re-Examination.* Larden: Macmillan.

Hegel, G. W. (1956). *Lectures on Philosophy of History (Trans. J. Sibree).* New York: Dover Publications.

_____(1977). *Hegel's Phenomenology of Spirit (Trans. A. V. Miller).* Oxford: Oxford University Press.

Lavine, T. Z. (1994). *From Socrates to Sartre: The Philosophic Quest.* New York: Bantam Books.

Lewis, M. H. (1997). Ancient Society, Research in Life, Lines, Human Progress from Savagery, Barbarianism to Civilization.

MacCarthy, F. (2000). *New Sunday and Holiday Liturgies.* Dublin: Dominican Publications.

Machiavelli, N. (1975). *The Prince.* Hammondsworth: Penguine Books.

Maclntrye, A. (1972). *Hegel.* New York: Doubleday.

Mill, J. S. (1948). *Essay on Liberty and Considerations on Representative Government.* Oxford: Basil Blackwell.

Miller, D. (1985). *Popper Selections.* Princeton: Princeton University Press.

Mure, G. R. (1965). *The Philosophy of Hegel.* London: Oxford University Press.

Nisbet, R. (1973). *The Social Philosophers: Community and Conflict in Western Thought.* New York: Thomas, Y. Crowell.

Peter, L. (1960). *John Locke Two Treatise on Government.* Cambridge: Cambridge University Press.

Plamenatz, J. (1992). *Man and Society: Political and Social Theories from Machiavelli to Marx.* London: Longman.

Plato. (1960). *The Laws.* London: Dent.

Plato. (1987). *Republic.* Middlesex: Penguine.

Popkin, H. R. (1991). *Philosophy made Simple (2nd ed.).* London: Butterworth-Heinemann Ltd.

Popper, K. (2002). *The Open Society and Its Enemies.* London: Routledge.

Presley, S. a. (2005). *Exquisite Rebel: The Essays of Voltaire de Cleyre- Anarchist, Feminist, Genius.* Albany: State University of New York Press.

Reyburn, H. A. (1921). *The Ethical Theory of Hegel.* Oxford: Oxford University Press.

Robert, E. G. (1993). *A Companion to Contemporary Political Philosophy.* Oxford: Basil Blackwell Ltd.

Rorty, R. (1992). *Heiddeger: A Critical Reader.* Cambridge: Basil Blackwell Ltd.

Russel, B. (1972). *A History of Western Philosophy.* London: Simon & Schuster.

Russel, B. (1972). *The Problems of Philosophy.* Oxford: Oxford University Press.

Schumpeter, J. (1950). *Capitlaism, Socialism and Democracy (3rd. ed.).* New York: Harper and Row.

Schutz, A. (1974). *The Structure of the Lifeworld: Hegel's Phenomenology of Spirit and Philosophy of Right.* Manchester: Manchester University Press.

Seymour, L. M. (1992). *Te Encyclopaedia of Democracy, Vol. 3.* New Delhi: Anmol Publications.

Seymour, L. M. (1995). *The Encyclopeadia of Democracy, Vol. 3.* London: Routledge.

Simon, F. (1964). *Hegel's Political Writings.* Oxford: Clarendon Press.

Sinha, C. (1992). *Anmol's Dictionary of Philosophy.* New Delhi: Anmol Publications.

Socrates, Book VIII. (n.d.).

Steinkraus, W. E. (1971). *New Studies in Hegel's Philosophy.* New York: Holt, Rinehart & Winston.

Stumpf, S. E. (1994). *Philosophy, History and Problems (5th Ed.).* New York: Oxford University Press.

Taylor, C. (1975). *Hegel.* London: Cambridge University Press.

The Annual Survey of Political Rights and Civil Liberties. (2006). *Freedom In the The World,* 50-62.

Tinker, I. (. (1990). *Persistent Inequalities.* New York: Oxford University Press.

Ullmann, W. (1966). *The Individual and Society in the Middle Ages.* Baltmore: John Hopkins University.

Ullmann, W. (1977). *Mediaval Foundations of Renaissance Humanism.* London: Elek Books.

Walliam, H. (1969). *The Intellectual Powers of Man.* Massachusetts: Massachusetts University Press.

Walsh, M. (1985). *A History of Philosophy.* London: Geoffrey Chapman.

Watt, I. (1959). *The Rise of the Novel: Studies in Defoe, Richardson and Fielding.* Berkeley : University of California Press.

Weinberg, J. (1960). *An Examination of Logical Positivism.* New Jersey: Littlefield Adams.

Weitz, M. (1967). *Philosophical Analysis: In Encyclopedia of Philosophy (Vol. 1& 2, Paul Edwards ed.).* London: Collier Macmillan.

Printed in the United States
By Bookmasters